The Easy Curry Cookbook

Anita Patel

CONTENTS

Welcome to this first physical book by Anita Patel. Other titles are available on Kindle and are as follows:-

Great Indian Vegetarian Cooking tips and recipes

Super Indian Snack and Streetfood recipes

Super Indian dessert recipes

Introduction

The object of this book is to show you how you can make a delicious Indian curry in only a few minutes. Once you have mastered these few basic principles you will be able to create your own dishes and put a meal on your table that will impress your family and friends, without having to spend the day in the kitchen. Unlike many other types of meal preparation quantities are not precise. When preparing Indian food it is better to feel, smell and taste, and you very soon understand how much of each spice to use. In the recipe section any quantities are just a guide and they have served me well over the years, but with trial and error you will soon find out how much of each spice to use in order to suit your taste.

There appears to be a great deal of mystique in the making of delicious Indian curries. There are many recipe books on the market with wonderful glossy photographs and if you follow the recipes you will get a tasty dish at the end. You will however have put in a huge amount of time and effort to achieve that result which often doesn't look like the picture. You will have been using a myriad of spices and adding them at certain times in very specific quantities. To many, it all seems so complicated and long winded.

The Indian housewife housewife however does not have these problems with her everyday cooking. She uses a few ingredients and can prepare a delicious meal in about 15 minutes.

This book will hopefully show you how you can do the same. The object of is to give a the reader a greater understanding of the use of spices and acquire the art of producing tasty Indian food.

To begin an adventure into Indian food it is worth equipping yourself with certain spices. If you do not have a convenient local Asian store then there are plenty of businesses online who will be able to provide you with the spices that you need. You will need a selection of both whole and ground spices and once you have them in stock they should last for a while. My advice to Indian cooks is to have a box or tray with all your spices in it to keep them in one place. When you start cooking curries all you have to do is get the box from the shelf and away you go. The list is not exhaustive but will enable you to cook a great number of great dishes.

Spices

Cumin

Cumin is an aromatic spice with a distinctive bitter taste and has a good oil content. It comes in several forms but the white and black cumin are the most common. It is widely used in Indian cuisine as well as North African, Mediterranean and Mexican cuisines. I recommend you stock cumin in both whole seed and ground forms.

Coriander

Coriander is very widely used in all its forms. Coriander comes from the parsley family and the seed is used whole and in the ground form. The leaves too are extensively used in Indian cooking. The seed has a lovely soft lemony flavour. The leaves when added to a curry at the end of cooking add freshness and give dishes a lift.

Turmeric

Turmeric comes from the same family of ginger and is believed to be indigenous of India where it has long been cultivated not only as a spice but as a dye. The root is used as a spice and after harvesting is ground into a powder. Its bright yellow colour makes it quite recognisable and some will say that when you are adding turmeric to a dish you are adding a little bit of the soil of India. It is believed to have medicinal properties.

Ginger

Ginger is native to Asia and its root is widely used in cooking where it is either grated or added in ground form. It is very pungent and has a distinctive taste. As well as being added to many Indian dishes it is widely used as a medicinal compound.

Chilli

The chilli is a native of the Americas and were introduced to Europe by Christopher Columbus and it was the Portuguese who brought the Chilli to India in the 16th century. It is used to provide flavour as well as heat to Indian food. It comes in various forms as the pepper itself fresh or dried and ground into chilli powder. The heat in chilli is created by the chemical capsicum which is eliminated by both milk and yoghurt, this being the reason yoghurt is used extensively in Indian cuisine.

Cardamom

Cardamom has a strong aromatic taste and comes in 2 forms black and green. The black cardamom has a more smoky flavour. Cardamom is usually added to dishes in pod form and is widely used in Indian sweet dishes. Green Cardamom has medicinal properties and in South America is used to treat a variety of ailments such as throat infections and congestion.

Cloves

Cloves originated in Indonesia and are a powerful spice often added to Indian meat dishes to add flavour. It goes well with cinnamon. Cloves are also often used to create sweet dishes and pairs well with apples and rhubarb. In the preparation of curries normally whole cloves are added.

Cinnamon

Cinnamon is the bark of the cassia tree. It has a

warm and aromatic citrous flavour. It is used to flavour curries and desserts and comes in the form of sticks or ground into powder. It is a constituent of garam masala.

Garam Masala

Garam Masala is a blend of ground spices and the composition can vary widely across the regions of India. There is no authentic mix of spices but the ones most widely used are black and white peppercorns, cloves, cinnamon, black and green cardamom pods and both black and white cumin seeds. Some commercial garam masala's may include ginger, turmeric, chilli, and mustard seeds. You can make your own by grinding a combination of whole spices in a grinder or a mortar and pestle.

Nigella

Nigella, also known as black cumin, onion seed and in India as Kalonji. It has quite a pungent and bitter taste. It is quite widely used as a spice in many Bengal dishes.

Asafoetida

Asafoetida is also known as devils dung and has an unpleasant smell when raw but is quite pleasant when used as a spice. It is used a lot in Bengali cuisine and is often used in conjunction with turmeric. It has a truffle like flavour when cooked.

Mustard Seed

This is the seed of the mustard plant and are often used as a whole seed by putting into hot oil until the pop and release their aroma.

Peppercorns

Pepper has been used to add heat to Indian foods since pre-history, long before the introduction of the chilli by the Portuguese. The peppercorn was a valuable commodity and often referred to as "black gold". White pepper is merely the husk of the black peppercorn removed.

Fenugreek

Fenugreek is an ancient spice which has a slightly bitter taste. It should be roasted to enable the seeds to pop and the oils to be released and is used mainly in the cooking of vegetables and dhals.

Panch Phoron

Panch phoron is a mixture of 5 whole spices, similar to Garam masala but using whole spices instead of ground. There are 5 spices, fenugreek seeds, nigella seeds, black mustard seeds, and cumin seeds. There are variations but this is the normal spice mix and the spices are mixed in equal quantities. It is widely used in Bengal cuisine.

5th Spice is fennel Seeds.

Basic Cooking Techniques

To make tasty curries you do not need to use a great number of spices in any Indian dish. In most cases only three will be used, a main spice along with a couple of others. Many Indian recipes are prepared to Ayurvedic principles which aims to achieve balance. We are thus trying to satisfy all the areas of taste which are sweet, salty, sour, bitter, pungent and astringent and whilst all recipes may not satisfy all six we are looking to achieve an overall balance. The dishes are trying to avoid the excessive sweetness or bitterness of so much western cooking these days. As an example, the addition of pungent spices can be more balancing to dishes using green leafy vegetables as you will discover later.

Vegetable Dishes

The first thing to do in starting to cook a vegetable dish is to heat up some oil in a pan or a wok. Once the oil is hot add the first spice. This is usually a seed and will affect the overall direction of your dish. For vegetable dishes normally either cumin seed, nigella seed, mustard seeds or panch phoron (see section on spices).

Add the seeds to the hot oil and wait until the seeds begin to crack. Once the seeds have begun to crack and release their aromatic oils add your vegetable. To the vegetable then add some ground turmeric and chilli powder, stir and then begin to cook the vegetable. The dish is now spiced.

We then need to consider finishing the dish and with vegetable dishes we have to consider the various areas of the tongue which are salt, sweet, sour, bitter and pungency. To to achieve this we consider adding salt, sugar, mustard paste, tomato and finally lemon. See the following example:-

Basic Bombay Potato

Start by cracking cumin seeds as your main spice. Once they have cracked add the potato (peeled and cut into small pieces). Follow this with turmeric and a touch of chilli powder to taste . To finish add a little tinned tomato, salt and a touch of sugar to sweeten. Once the potatoes are soft you have a basic but very acceptable Bombay potato dish.

Basic Cabbage curry

Here we shall use mustard seeds as the basic spice. Add oil and heat followed by mustard seeds. Once they have cracked put in the cabbage followed by turmeric and chilli powder. To finish try using mustard paste which really is good when used with leafy green vegetables like cabbage. Follow the mustard paste with a little salt and sugar. Once cooked you have another very acceptable cabbage dished cooked in an

Indian style. The above picture shows a basic cabbage curry with a few frozen peas added.

Meat Dishes

It is usual to begin meat dishes with the holy trinity of onion, ginger and garlic. Heat some oil in a pan and and finely chopped or minced onion, chopped garlic and either fresh or ground ginger and cook until the onion is beginning to soften and go translucent. Do try to avoid burning the onions.

Add the meat and follow by adding your spice which in most cases will be garam masala and a mixture of spices. Next add turmeric and some chilli powder as spice 2 and 3.

The finishing flavours then need to be added which could be tomato, yoghurt, crème fresh. Finally add salt and sugar to taste.

Basic Chicken Tikka Masala

Add oil to a pan and add onion ginger and garlic as above. Add some garam masala followed by turmeric and chilli powder or flakes. Add some tinned tomatoes followed by salt and sugar. Cook until the tomato has darkened and you can see the oil emerging through the tomato to the top. Add chicken pieces and simmer until the chicken is cooked through. Follow this with some crème fresh or yoghurt, stir in to give it that chicken tikka masala appearance.

A delicious dish cooked in about 15-20 minutes.

Serve with some bombay potato or another vegetable along with some naan bread.

If you wanted to finish the dish in another way instead of adding tomato, just add chicken after the onion, ginger and garlic and garam masala. Add chilli and turmeric and cook the chicken To finish add some crème fresh or yoghurt and maybe some ground almonds to give your dish a korma feel.

The above technique can be used with any meat and you can also add some additional spices if you want to enhance certain flavours.

As an example I would use lamb or beef. After the onion ginger garlic stage add the lamb followed by garam masala, chilli and turmeric and then add some cardamom seeds, cloves and a stick of cinnamon. Add yoghurt and seasoning and cook in a casserole until the meat is tender. To finish add some spinach, cook and reduce the liquid so that you have a relatively dry dish and serve with either rice or naan bread.

As you can see from the above few sentences you already have the basics for making several delicious curries. Once you become familiar with using spices you will know instinctively what to add to enhance flavours, so that you obtain the result that you want.

Recipe Ideas

Indian Cheese on Toast

Indian cheese on toast is a normal cheese on toast but prepared in the Indian style. It makes use of red onion, green chilli and ground coriander and this together with the bread and cheese will give a you a mouthwatering spicy snack. Any cheese that melts well will do. I would suggest a cheddar cheese but the choice is yours.

Ingredients

½ red onion finely chopped

1 tsp ground coriander

a handful fresh coriander

1 green chilli chopped

grated cheese

bread slices

Method

Put the grated cheese into a bowl and add all the

other ingredients. Put the mixture oto some toasted bread slices and melt under the grill. As the cheese melts you can add a little more so that you have wonderful heaped melted cheese mixture on top of your toast.

Indian Omelette

An omelette is often eaten as a light lunch dish in India and here is one variation using red onion, green chilli, tomato and coriander. The preparation has similarities with the Spanish Tortilla and the Italian Frittata but this Indian version has a bit of spice to it.

Ingredients

3 or 4 eggs

1/2-1 red onion chopped small.

1 tomato, chopped

1 green chilli, chopped

ground coriander

fresh coriander

fresh or ground ginger

oil

Method

Add oil to a frying pan and heat. Add the onion

and chilli and start to soften and caramelize. Add the ginger and tomato and allow this mixture to cook and the tomatoes to caramelize also.

Crack the eggs into a bowl and add 1tsp ground coriander, salt and fresh coriander and stir everything together.

Add to the pan with the onion and tomato and slowly cook the omelette, going round the edges folding them in and allowing liquid to take their place. Once the bottom is cooked finish the dish off by cooking the top under the grill or turning the omelette onto a plate and putting back into the pan to enable the reverse side to be cooked.

Serve.

Prawn curry

This is a very quick and tasty way to make a prawn curry. As prawns can be expensive I often substitute prawns for a white fish. It still tastes very good. The main spice for this dish and one which is used a lot for fish in Indian cooking is Nigella seeds

Ingredients

1lb Prawns shelled

About 1/2 tin of tomatoes

1 green chilli

1 tsp nigella seeds

1tsp turmeric

A bit of chilli powder or flakes to taste

Watered down English mustard paste

salt

sugar

fresh coriander leaves

Oil

Method

Heat the oil in a pan and add the nigella seeds and cook until they start cracking. Add the green chilli just broken into half. The chilli is not to add heat but to give the dish freshness and flavour. Add the tomatoes and cook. What you are looking for is for the oil to come up through the tomatoes and wait until the tomatoes start to caramelize. It is important to do this as we want to bring out the flavours so take a bit of time here.

Add the turmeric and chilli powder. The chilli powder is there to add flavour other than heat. Stir the spices in.

The sauce will thicken and the edges should go a deep red. At this stage add a little watered down mustard paste. Add some salt and a little sugar.

Ensure everything is cooked and well combined and add the prawns.

As the prawns are cooked you just need to heat through otherwise the prawns will go rubbery.

To finish add a handful of fresh coriander to add freshness.

Cabbage Curry

This recipe will transform a humble Savoy cabbage into something very delicious and I would urge you to try this very easy recipe.

Ingredients

Savoy cabbage chopped

1 tsp mustard seeds

1 tsp turmeric

½ tsp chilli or more to taste.

Mustard paste

Salt

Sugar

Squeeze of lemon

Method

Heat oil in a pan or a wok and add the mustard seeds. Cook the seeds until they pop and crackle.

Add the cabbage along with the turmeric and chilli

Stir fry until the cabbage is cooked.

To finish add some mustard paste salt and a little sugar and stir in.

Right at the end add a squeeze of lemon juice to finish.

Serve.

As a variation try adding a bit of tomato instead of the lemon. By doing this you can provide different dishes with a limited range of ingredients. Play around until you find one you like.

Leek Curry

This is a wonderful way to cook leeks and the make a great side dish or part of a selection of dishes. It is also very easy and only takes a few minutes.

Ingredients

2 or 3 Leeks cut into slices

1 tsp Nigella seeds

1 tsp chilli powder or flakes to taste

1 tsp turmeric

Pinch of salt

1 tsp sugar

Squeeze of lemon

Oil

A few dried chick peas fried in oil. (optional)

Method

Heat oil in a pan or wok. Add the nigella seeds and heat until they start popping.

Add the leeks and toss them into the spiced oil.

Add the turmeric and chilli

Once the leeks are soft add the salt and the sugar

Finally add a squeeze of lemon.

As a variation take a few fried dry chick peas to the pan (not tinned which are cooked). They add a nutty texture which can make a pleasant change.

Potato and bean curry

This type of dish is very quick and easy to prepare, is quite delicious and normally used as a side dish or as part of a meal containing a number of dishes. The beans may be substituted by using peas or mushrooms. As in all theses dishes the quantities are not written in tablets. Experiment to find the balance that you like.

Ingredients

2 or 3 Potatoes peeled and cut into small bite sized chunks

A handful Green beans, if they along cut into

smaller lengths

1 tsp Cumin seeds

½ tsp Turmeric

1tsp Chilli powder or flakes

lemon juice

Oil

Salt

Method

Par-boil the potatoes and blanch the beans

Heat some oil in a frying pan or wok. When hot add the cumin seeds and wait until the start to pop.

Add the potatoes and fry until the begin to just colour

Add the beans along with the chilli and turmeric and salt. Stir in and continue cooking until the potatoes are fried and the beans have softened.

Add a splash of lemon juice and continue cooking

for another minute.

When the potatoes are cooked through the dish is ready

Garnish with fresh coriander and serve.

Courgette Curry

This is a super way of cooking courgettes just like it would be cooked in an Indian household. There is no chilli in this dish, but if you would like some heat then add 1 or 2 whole green chillies at the beginning when you put in your spices. This is not a complicated dish to prepare and within a 15 minutes you can have this on the table ready to eat.

Ingredients

2 Courgettes

1tsp Fenugreek seeds

1tsp Asafoetida

Oil

Salt

Sugar

Squeeze of lemon

Method

Heat a little oil in a pan or wok and add the

fenugreek seeds. Be careful with them as they do burn easily when they start popping add the asafoetida followed by the courgettes.

Allow the courgettes to start to soften and add the 3rd spice which is turmeric and allow the courgettes to cook.

To finish add salt to taste and assist in the release of liquid, add some sugar and a squeeze of lemon.

Serve with chappatis or naan.

Mixed Vegetable Curry

Whilst I am using spinach for this example you can use any leafy vegetable and achieve good results. Whilst spinach is the main vegetable you also use potato, mooli and aubergine making a lovely mixed vegetable dish. If you don't have mooli then just leave it out.

Ingredients

1tsp Panch phoron (if you don't have, use cumin or mustard seed)

2 red whole chillies1 or 2 Potato peeled and cubed

1 Mooli cubed

1 aubergine cubed

½ lb (250gm) Spinach

1 tsp turmeric

1tsp chilli powder to taste

Salt to taste

1 tsp sugar

2-3 tsp watered down mustard paste

Oil

Method

Heat the oil in a pan and once hot add the panch phoron and wait until the seeds start to pop.

Add the whole chilli

Add the potatoes and start to brown and follow with the mooli and aubergine. Allow the vegetables to start to soften.

Add the Spinach along with turmeric and chilli powder.

Allow the spinach to wilt and and add salt and a little sugar.

To finish stir in the watered down mustard paste

Serve with naan bread or rice.

How to make a basic dahl

Dahls are widely eaten in India and are very versatile. They can be served as a main course, a side dish or even made into a soup. There is quite large range of different dahls and red lentils are a good way to start on the road of making a dahl. A dish of dahl can be a wonderful warming "comfort food". Delicious.

Ingredients

1 cup of red lentils washed

2 cups of water

1 tsp turmeric

tin of tomatoes

To Finish

Ghee or butter

1-2 tsp cumin seeds

Green chilli chopped

Salt

A little sugar

fFesh coriander or lemon zest

A squeeze of lemon at the end

Method

Add the water, tomatoes and turmeric to the lentils, bring to the boil and allow to boil. The lentils will become a mush once they are cooked.

Put the lentils to one side.

In a separate pan or wok add the ghee or tuber and melt. Put the cumin seeds into the butter and allow to crack and release their spices. Add the chopped chilli. Once the cumin seeds are ready and have browned add the dahl.

At this stage decide whether you want the dahl more liquid or thicker. Add water to thin and just evaporate water to thicken.

Add salt, a little sugar and some fresh coriander to lift the dish. You could use some grated lemon zest as an alternative if you wish. Finally just add a squeeze of lemon.

How to cook Perfect rice

Cooking perfect rice seems to cause difficulties for many people yet it really can be quite easy if you follow a few basic steps. The main one one is to use us 1 part of rice to 2 parts water

Ingredients

I cup of rice

2 cups of water

Salt if used

Method

Rinse the rice through several times with cold water to remove excess starch.

Put the rice into a pan and add the water. Bring

to the boil and as soon as the water starts to reduce take of the heat and put a lid on the pan.

Leave for about 10 minutes and you should then have well cooked rice.

How to make fried rice

This can be served as a side dish or it could be served as a light lunch. Here we change the texture somewhat by frying the rice in spiced oil for a few minutes and adding some vegetables.

Ingredients

I cup of rice

2-3 cups of water

Oil

Assorted vegetables such as chopped carrots, some peas and maybe broccoli including stems.

2 tsp mustard seeds

Method

Rinse the rice several times in cold water to get rid of excess starch

Heat the oil in a pan or wok and once hot add the mustard seeds and cook until they start to crackle.

Add the vegetables and fry with the spices and

caramelise a little.

Add the rice and cover the rice grains with the oil. The rice will go slightly glossy and be mixed with the mustard seed.

Add the water and bring to the boil. As with the boiled rice recipe once it boils and the liquid starts to reduce take of the heat and put a lid on the pan.

Leave for 10 minutes when the rice should be cooked.

How to cook Rice with Dill and Mustard seed

If you are looking for an different way to serve rice then why not try this. Rice with dill is rice cooked with some spices with the addition of some dill. The recipe also uses a couple of black cardamom pods which gives the rice an aromatic flavour. If you want the dish to have an "Indian restaurant yellow colour then add a little turmeric when you add the water. Instead of using mustard seeds you could also use cumin seeds.

Ingredients

1 large cup of rice

2-3 cups of water

2 tsp of mustard seeds

2 Black cardamom seeds

Oil

Salt

A handful of dill

Method

Put oil in a pan and heat. Add the mustard seeds and allow them to crack. Add a couple of black cardamom pods to the pan and allow to fry in the oil for a minute or so and add the rice and salt if used.

Stir around to coat the rice grains with the oil.

Add the dill and stir into the rice.

Add the water to rice and bring the water to the boil. Once the water has been absorbed take of the heat put the lid on the pan and let the pan rest for 10 minutes.

The rice should be perfectly cooked.

Keema and peas

Keema is a wonderful Indian dish, one I use very much as a stand by. Its main ingredient is minced meat. In India lamb would normally be used as Hindus do not eat beef, but you can use beef for this recipe and it works just as well. This is one of the many mince dishes from throughout the world, Mexico has its chilli, Italy as bolognaise sauce, UK has mince and dumplings and Scandinavia has meat balls.

Keema is not difficult to prepare and it is well worth cooking.

Ingredients

About 1lb minced beef or lamb

Garlic

1-2 tsp ginger

1 can of tomatoes

1/2-1 tsp turmeric

A whole green chilli

1-2 tsp chilli powder or flakes

1 tsp ground cinnamon and ground coriander (optional)

2-3 tsp garam masala

Peas

Salt.

Oil

Method

Peel and chop the onion ginger and garlic and fry gently in some heated oil to soften the onion.

You want it to be soft and transparent rather than brown.

Chop and add the green chilli, this adds some freshness to the dish. Add the garam masala. You can also add the cinnamon and coriander at this stage if you wish to enhance those flavours. It really does come down to taste and experience. Let it gently cook to allow the spices to release their flavours.

Add the tomatoes and mix in and gently cook whilst stirring. The tomatoes will lose their bright red colour and the oil will rise to the top. This is forming what is known as a masala. Once they are a rich brown colour add the meat.

Allow this mixture to cook for a while and then you can add the turmeric   and the chilli and some salt.

Once the meat is cooked through add the peas. Once they are cooked the dish is ready. Check the seasoning.

Serve garnished with fresh coriander.

Cauliflower and Potato Curry

This popular Indian dish also know as aloo gobi can be eaten as a light lunch with some Indian bread or as a side dish along with a selection of other dishes. Some people even use it as a sandwich filling!!.

Ingredients

Oil

1-2 tsp cumin seeds

1 tsp chilli powder or flakes

1 tsp turmeric

2 or 3 potatoes peeled and chopped into bite sized cubes

Cauliflower cut into pieces

Salt

Method

Heat the oil in a pan or wok. When hot as the cumin seeds and cook until they start to pop..

Add the potatoes along with the chilli and gently fry until the potatoes just start to go soft (about 5-7 minutes).

Add the cauliflower along with the turmeric and season with salt

Put a lid on the pan and gently cook until the potatoes and cauliflower are soft. Try not to add any water as this will affect the flavour of the finished dish, just cook slowly.

Pumpkin Bhaji

This is an easy recipe to make and can be enjoyed with some paratha or naan bread. It uses an almost equal quantity of both pumpkin and onions and it is worth ensuring that the onions are well caramelized as this will give a dish a wonderful sweetness.

Ingredients

Pumpkin

2-3 large onions peeled and chopped

A couple of fresh chillies chopped

1 tsp cumin seeds

1/2-1 tsp ground turmeric.

Sugar

Salt

Oil

Method

Heat oil in a pan and put in the cumin seeds and chillies and fry the seeds until they crack and pop.

Add the onion fry for several minutes whilst stirring. Ensure that they start to caramelise. Add the pumpkin and turmeric and stir in.

Add salt and sugar and cook until the pumpkin is cooked but still firm. This is a dry dish and we do not want the pumpkin to be mushy.

Serve with naan or roti or as a side dish.

Aubergine and Tomato Bhaji – Tomato begun

This dish can be eaten as a snack with naan or roti or as a side dish. Not difficult to prepare and quite delicious. You could substitute the 3 whole spices with panch phoron if you wish.

Ingredients

1 aubergine (eggplant) cut into cubes

1 large tomato diced

1 tsp cumin seeds

1tsp fennel seeds

1 tsp nigella seeds

Chopped garlic

Chilli powder or flakes

1tsp ground cumin

Salt

Fresh coriander chopped

Method

Heat oil in a pan and add the nigella seeds, cumin seeds and fennel seeds and cook until they splutter and pop.

Add the aubergine and tomato and cook until the aubergine begins to soften.

Add the chilli flakes, cumin and salt and finish cooking the aubergine.

Stir in fresh coriander

Serve.

Pan Roasted Panch Phoron Potatoes

This is a basic way of roasting potatoes and other vegetables in India and is quick and easy to do.

Ingredients

Vegetable oil

2-3 tsp panch phoron

About 1lb new or small cut potatoes either whole or halved depending on the size you want.

¼ tsp asafoetida

Salt

Juice of ½ lemon.

Method

Heat oil in a pan and when hot add the panch phoron and cook until the seeds begin to crack and pop and put in the potatoes.

Add the asafoetida and stir together and lightly fry for about 5 minutes.

Add a cup of water, cover and cook covered until

the potatoes are just tender.

Remove the lid and roast the potatoes in the pan until they are browned and any excess liquid is evaporated.

Season with salt and add the lemon juice.

Serve warm, at room temperature, or cold.

Pumpkin and Spinach Curry

You can also prepare this using bitternut squash and is an extremely tasty vegetable dish that is quick and easy to prepare.

Ingredients

Pumpkin or squash chopped

Some chopped spinach leaves.

Small onion chopped

1tsp ground ginger

1 tsp panch phoron

½ tsp chilli powder to taste

½ tsp turmeric

Salt

Oil

Method

Heat oil in a pan, add the panch phoron and cook until the seeds crack and pop.

Add the onion and ginger, cook gently until it softens and begins to caramelize

Add the pumpkin along with the turmeric and chilli and cook gently covered until it begins to soften. Add a little water if the pumpkin starts to stick. Be careful though as the spinach will be holding have a lot of moisture.

Once the pumpkin begins to soften add the spinach leaves and cook for 5 minutes or until your vegetables are cooked but the pumpkin is not mushy.

Serve

Chicken Tikka

Chicken Tikka is very much a traditional Indian dish eaten widely throughout India and Pakistan. Is is also one of those dishes that has gained popularity all over the world. It is one of those dishes that I prepare and eat regularly as it is a healthy option, is quick and easy to make and is not expensive. The word tikka literally means bits and the dish essentially is chicken pieces that have been marinated in yoghurt and spices and cooked in a clay oven known as a Tandoor. The oven is cylindrical in shape and the heat is provided by burning wood or charcoal. The cooking in a tandoor is radiant from the burning coals, convection from the air passing around and of course smoking from the smoke caused as fat drips onto the coals. As most homes do not have a tandoor cooking may be done either in a conventional oven or under the grill. It is also a good dish to be produced on a barbecue.

To prepare chicken tikka you will need the following ingredients:-

1 kg (2.2lb) chicken thighs de-skinned

250ml (1/2 pint) natural yoghurt

1 tsp chilli powder to taste

2tsp ground ginger

1tsp garlic paste or powder

2tsp garam masala powder

1/2tsp salt

¼ tsp red food colouring

Juice of 1 lemon

Oil

Method

Put the ginger, garlic, garam masala, salt and food colouring into the yoghurt and mix. Put the chicken thighs into the yoghurt and allow to marinate for about 30 minutes.

Put the coated chicken on a rack and cook in the oven turning from time until the chicken is cooked and it is golden brown.

You can serve with wedges of lemon, a green salad, Naan bread or any other Indian bread and some Chutney. I sometimes serve with a lentil and tomato dish shown on this site.

Enjoy!

Lamb Dhania (Lamb with coriander)

This is a special dish, a little more complicated than previous recipes but not too difficult and building on the blocks laid down in previous dishes. This is quite quick to prepare and makes an excellent dinner party dish. It is also a little more expensive to prepare but the lamb can be substituted for chicken. Go ahead and impress your family and friends by cooking them an Indian feast.

Ingredients

About 450 gms 1lb lamb (shoulder is fine) fat removed and cut into bite sized cubes.

1 or 2 large handfuls of fresh coriander

2 or 3 fresh green chillies

8-10 unsalted cashew nuts

1 tsp cumin seeds

1-2 tsp each ginger and garlic paste

1-2 tsp ground coriander

½ tsp turmeric

Salt to taste

3-4 tablespoonsful of natural yoghurt.

Oil

Method

Blend the coriander leaves, chillies, cashew nuts together in a blender along with a little water until you have a fine paste.

Heat some oil in a pan and add the cumin seeds and cook until they crack. Add the ginger and garlic paste, turmeric and ground coriander and cook to combine for a minute or two and add the coriander paste mixture.

Cook gently for about 5 minutes until the oil starts to come up through the paste. Add the lamb along with the yoghurt. Season with a little salt

Stir the mixture to combine, cover and simmer until the lamb is cooked.

If you want a dry dish then remove the lid and let the liquid evaporate to the required consistency. Alternatively this could be served with a little of the gravy to make it a wetter dish. The choice is yours.

Serve with either rice or some naan or rotis.

Brussel Sprout curry

If you have some brussel sprouts left over from Christmas or you happen to like sprouts here is a recipes to tickle the taste buds. You could use this recipe as part of an Indian feast with other dishes or you could use it alongside some cold turkey after Christmas. This is a great recipe using either fresh or left over sprouts. It uses those wonderful nuggets in the spice mix panch phoron and some salted cashew nuts at the end give this dish and added texture.

Ingredients

Sprouts either fresh or left over. If fresh I would recommend par boiling.

Oil

1 tsp Panch Phoron

1/2-1 tsp chilli powder

1 tsp turmeric

Squeeze of lemon juice

Salt

Sugar

Salted cashew nuts (optional)

Method

Heat Oil in a pan and when hot add the panch phoron. Do not have the oil too hot as you do not want the seeds burning.

Add the sprouts along with the chilli powder and turmeric and stir in.

Fry the mixture until the sprouts are at the texture you want, I don't like them too soft.

To finish add the lemon juice, salt and sugar.

Finally, if using add the cashew nuts which give the dish an added texture.

Mix and serve.

8038421R10044

Printed in Great Britain
by Amazon.co.uk, Ltd.,
Marston Gate.